WHO CONQUERED MOUNT EVEREST?

AMAZING FACTS BOOK FOR KIDS
CHILDREN'S NATURE BOOKS

BABY PROFESSOR
EDUCATION KIDS

In this book, we're going to talk about who conquered Mount Everest. So, let's get right to it!

WHERE IS MOUNT EVEREST?

Rising from the beautiful Himalayan Mountain Range is the majestic Mount Everest, which is the tallest mountain in the world. It rises 29,035 feet skywards and is located in the Sagarmatha Zone, which is in the country of Nepal where Nepal, China, and Tibet meet.

MOUNT EVEREST

GROUP OF CLIMBERS REACHING THE SUMMIT

This mountain has challenged many climbers and it was 1953 before the first successful climb was made. To date, more than 600 people have attempted to reach the peak and many have died trying. The mountain has claimed the lives of at least 100 climbers.

CONQUERING MOUNT EVEREST

Many people believed that Mount Everest would never be conquered. Before the summit was reached, there were other expeditions that almost made it there. Perhaps the most famous took place in 1924. During this climb, George Leigh Mallory was one of the climbers and Andrew "Sandy" Irvine was the other. They were last seen at a height of about 28,000 feet and no one knows if they ever made it to the top or not since they never made it down the mountain.

THE DANGERS OF MOUNT EVEREST

Although it isn't considered the most difficult mountain in the world to climb today, there are many dangerous conditions that climbers attempting to scale Mount Everest encounter. The freezing temperatures mean that climbers are always at a risk for frostbite. They can fall off cliffs to their deaths or into jagged crevasses.

Climbers can also succumb to altitude sickness beginning from about 8,000 feet and higher. Because the altitude is so high, enough oxygen doesn't get to the brain causing a feeling of sickness called hypoxia.

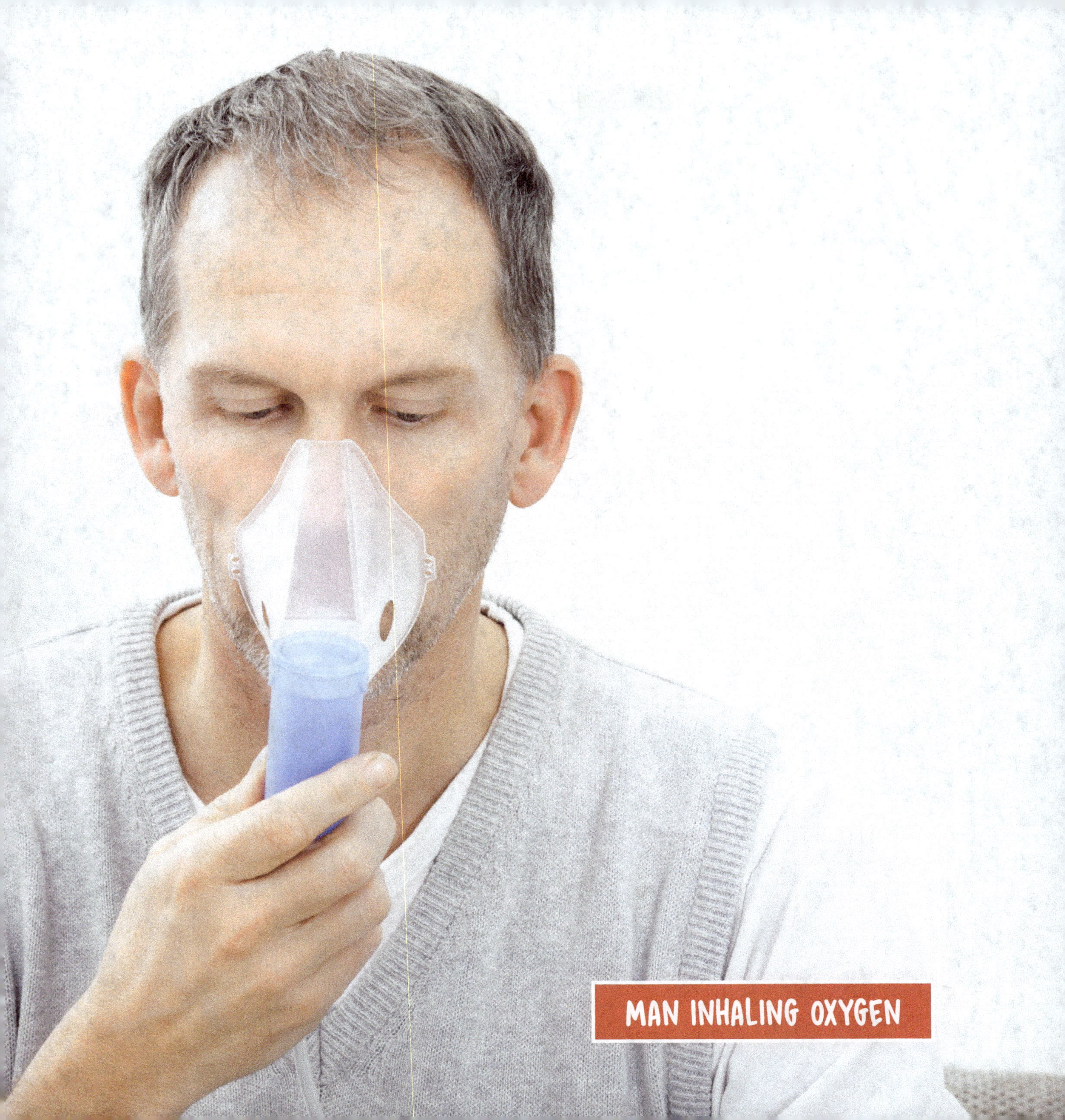

MAN INHALING OXYGEN

INSOMNIA

Even if a person survives hypoxia, he or she can suffer permanent brain damage. During a climb, people have experienced headaches, fuzzy thinking, insomnia, loss of appetite, and intense fatigue. Even more acute than these symptoms are the symptoms of dementia, difficulty with coordination including trouble walking, and even hallucinations or coma.

To prevent this physical trauma from happening, climbers take time, sometimes many weeks, to climb up the mountain so they can give their bodies a chance to get used to the severe change in altitude.

MAN EATING LUNCH

GETTING ADEQUATE FOOD AND SUPPLIES

Not many animals or plants survive in the high altitudes of the Himalayas. Since there are really no natural food sources, expeditions need to plan, buy, and then haul all their needed food and supplies up the mountain.

Most climbing teams hire Sherpas to help them. Sherpas are a population of nomads who have adapted to the high altitudes. Without the Sherpas and other guides from Nepal, successful climbs wouldn't be possible.

WHO WAS PART OF THE FIRST SUCCESSFUL EXPEDITION?

In the year 1953, the British government received word that the country of Nepal would allow them to make an expedition to Mount Everest. At that time, only one expedition was given approval for an entire calendar year.

The expedition's leader was John Hunt and he requested that Edmund Hillary join the group. Hunt had selected expert climbers as well as a filmmaker, a writer, and a physiologist to go on the expedition.

EDMUND HILLARY

Hillary was a climber from New Zealand who had been fascinated by mountain climbing since he was 16 years of age. He had scaled his first mountain at the age of 20. Hillary was ready to conquer Everest.

In order to carry the needed food and supplies, a large group of people was necessary. There were over 400 people in the group. They planned to climb the massive mountain in stages so they could get used to the high altitude.

ARRIVING AT TENGPOCHE MONASTERY

On March 26, 1953, the expedition reached Tengpoche Monastery at the base of the mountain. It had taken them over two weeks to get there. They hiked up the hot Katmundu Valley first. The terrain on the way was level and the team was very excited about the approaching mountain peak.

The Sherpas, the population of nomadic peoples from Nepal who believe the mountain is sacred, were witnessing the event and joined the expedition to celebrate their arrival at the monastery. The members of the expedition set up their rear camp at this location, which is 12,887 feet above sea level.

KHUMBU ICEFALL

ARRIVING AT BASE CAMP

On April 12, 1953, Edmund Hillary led some members of the expedition up the slippery glacier called Khumbu Icefall. Getting up the icefall was a very difficult climb and tested the training of all concerned. This was the location where the group had planned to set up Base Camp, but it was difficult to do so with the jagged edges of ice and the barren landscape.

However, they succeeded and then set up eight different relay camps with food and shelter "at the ready." The group moved from camp to camp as they got prepared for the final treacherous climb. At this point in their journey, they were about 17,980 feet above sea level.

TENZING NORGAY

ARRIVING AT CAMP IV

They arrived at Camp IV on April 26, 1953. On their way to the camp, which was 21,280 feet above sea level, Hillary and his teammate and Sherpa guide, Tenzing Norgay, cut steps out of the ice on the mountain. They were tied together with ropes as they carefully maneuvered around deep crevasses in the Earth masked by snow and ice.

After hours of toil, they got to Camp IV and began to go back down to Base Camp. Then, something very scary happened. Hillary jumped on what appeared to be a sturdy block of ice, but it was loose. The ice block fell off the mountain and took Hillary for a dangerous ride.

Norgay quickly grabbed the rope and saved Hillary. Without Norgay's quick action, Hillary would more than likely not have survived. Their teamwork proved to be successful throughout the perilous journey.

ARRIVING AT SOUTH COL

On May 26, the team had been at South Col, which was also called Camp VIII, for about a month. This location at 26,080 feet above sea level was the last major ridge they had to climb before they reached the summit of Mount Everest. Team member Tom Bourdillon and his teammate Charles Evans were given the go-ahead to begin the final summit.

SOUTH COL

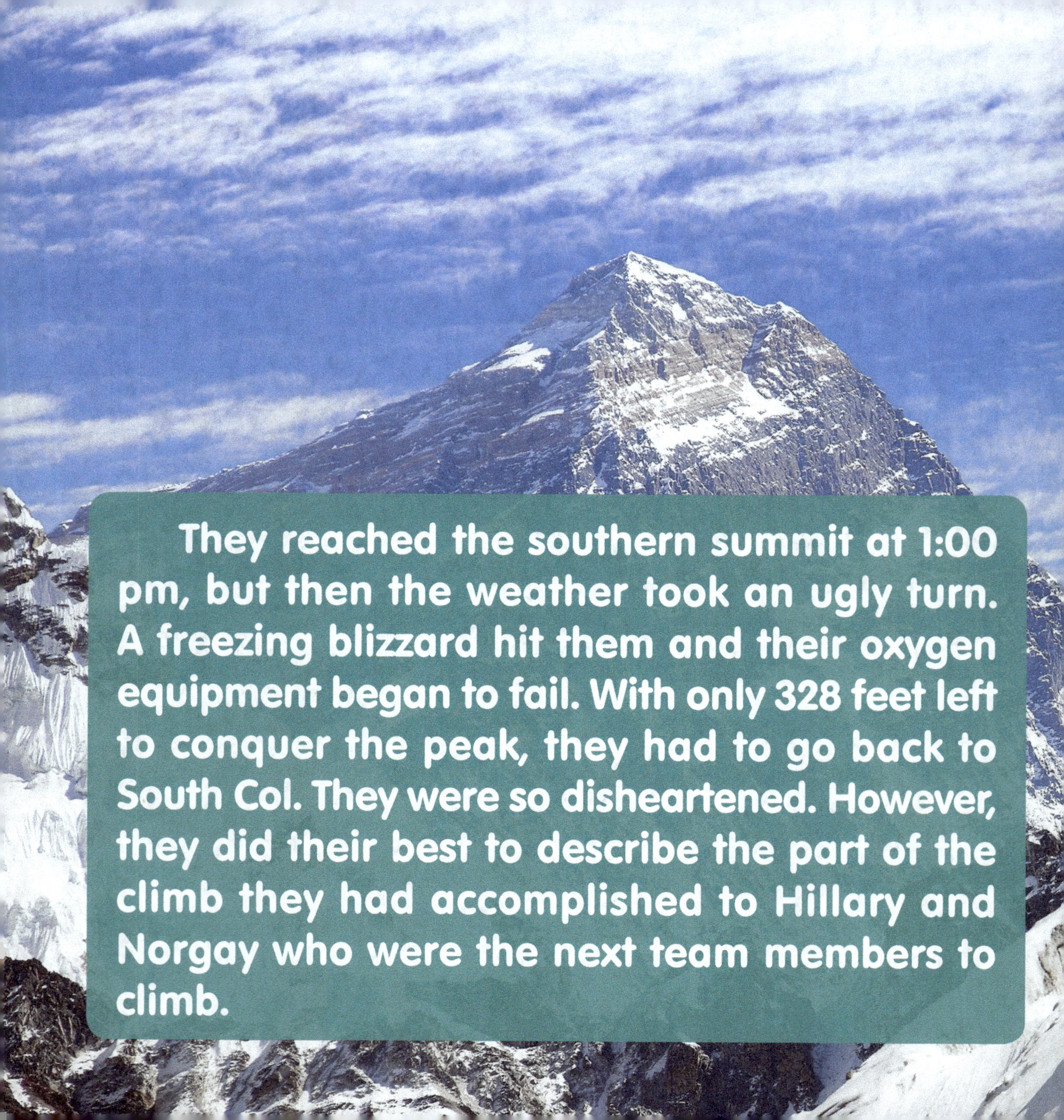

They reached the southern summit at 1:00 pm, but then the weather took an ugly turn. A freezing blizzard hit them and their oxygen equipment began to fail. With only 328 feet left to conquer the peak, they had to go back to South Col. They were so disheartened. However, they did their best to describe the part of the climb they had accomplished to Hillary and Norgay who were the next team members to climb.

ARRIVING AT CAMP IX

On May 28, after the team helped Hillary and Norgay set up Camp IX, they left to go back down the mountain. The two men had a tent set up on a slanted slope. They tried to eat something to get their strength up even though the altitude of 27,900 above sea level prevented them from having much of an appetite.

CANNED SARDINES

They ate canned sardines along with biscuits and jam as well as soup and coffee. The wind chill and below-freezing temperature in addition to strong winds, made their night almost unbearable.

ARRIVING AT THE SUMMIT

The next day, the two men were ready to go at 4:30 am, but there was a problem. Hillary's boots were totally frozen and it took them about two hours to thaw them out. As soon as they were thawed, they strapped on their crampons, which are spikes for maneuvering on ice, and they set off.

CRAMPONS

They were faced with a vertical cliff of ice and snow measuring over 40 feet high. They had to use every ounce of their remaining energy to cut ice steps out of the frozen mountain with their ice picks. As soon as they climbed over one ridge, they were faced with another.

Finally, they had reached the very top! At 11:30 am, on May 29, 1953, they conquered the mighty mountain. They stepped atop the summit. Hillary took photos and Norgay planted an axe into the ice with the flags of his country, Nepal, as well as the flags of Great Britain, India, and the United Nations.

They both looked out over the expansive peaks and valleys and considered themselves lucky to have made it there alive. They were the first people to ever see the view from the top of Everest. They stayed there for a mere 15 minutes, but it didn't matter because they were both famous and went on to conquer many more mountains in their lifetimes. The two men made a pact not to reveal who had actually stepped up on the summit first, but it was later revealed that it was Hillary. The two men had achieved their dream.

CLIMBING MOUNT EVEREST'S PEAK

Over the centuries, many men and women have dreamed of climbing to the top of Mount Everest. The first men to reach the summit after a perilous, difficult climb were Edmund Hillary and Tenzing Norgay on the 29th of May in 1953.

Awesome! Now that you've read about who conquered Mount Everest, you may want to read more about the highest mountains in the world in the Baby Professor book The Highest Mountains in The World – Geology for Children.